Jafta—My Mother

Story by Hugh Lewin
Pictures by Lisa Kopper

Evans Brothers Limited London

I would like you, said Jafta, to meet my mother.
There is nobody I know quite like my mother.

My mother is like the earth —
full of goodness, warm and brown and strong.

My mother is like the sun rising
in the early morning,
lighting up the dark corners
and gently coaxing us awake.
She prods the fire into life
and soon everywhere is filled
with the smoky smell of food,
bringing rumbles to my tummy
and making me want to get up.

As the sun starts its day
and the flowers burst open
to turn and follow it
across the sky,
I think of my mother.

Like the sky, she's always there.
You can always look up
and see her.

At midday when the sun is high and strongest,
she shades and comforts us,
like the willows on the bank of the river.

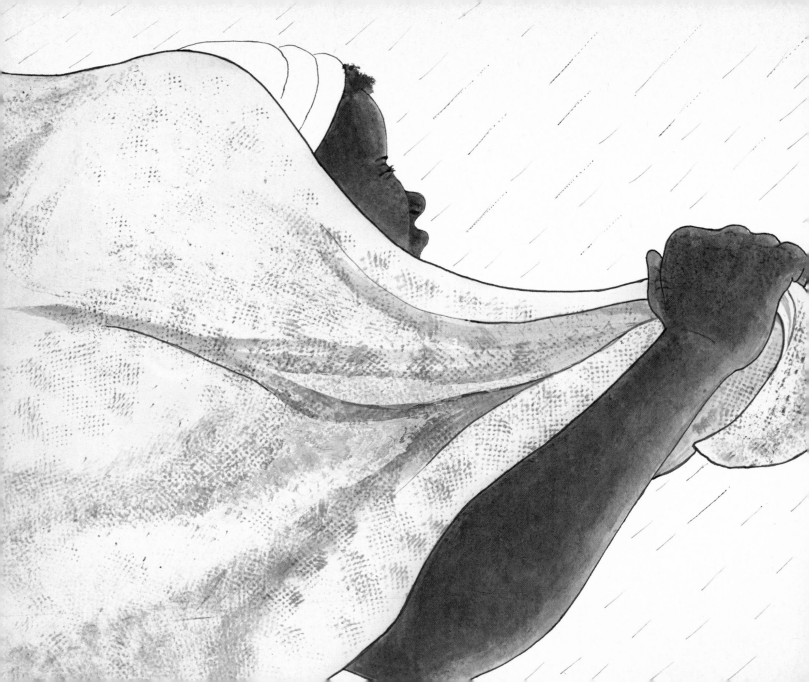

Or when the day has become too hot and stuffy,
she cools us as the rain does
when it turns the dust-bowls into rippling puddles,
washing out the grass and making it green again.

She doesn't often complain,
even in the bad times.

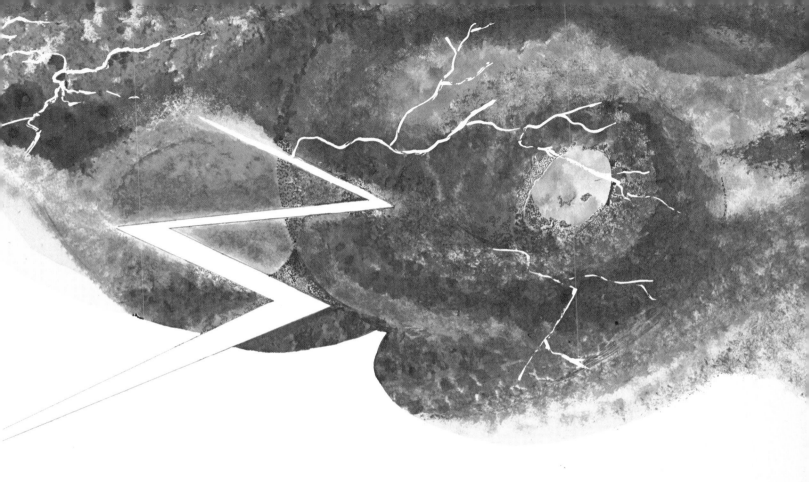

But beware! If she finds you cheating at a game,
or teasing your younger sisters,
she can sound like thunder in the afternoon
and her eyes will flash
like the lightning out of the dark clouds.

My mother doesn't often storm, said Jafta,
and it's much nicer when she sings.
  She sings to us
   as she cooks the evening meal.
    If you've heard a hoopoe call
     across the mealies,
      you've heard my mother sing.

After supper it's time for the stories. Somehow,
said Jafta, I think I almost love my mother best then —

after the food and the hurrying, when the sun's going down and everything's quieter and cooler.

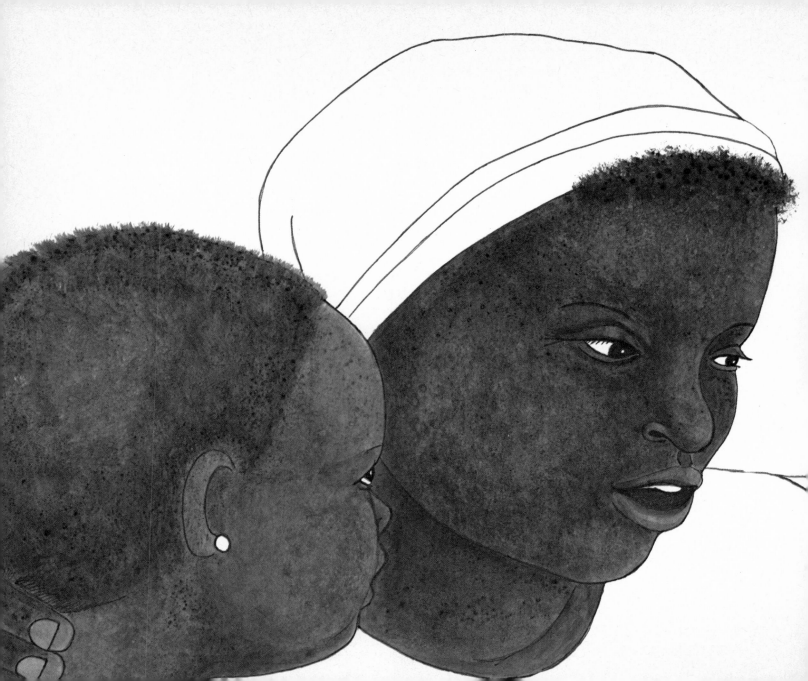

Then she hugs us round her and chases away our sadnesses.
We talk about today, and yesterday,
and especially tomorrow.

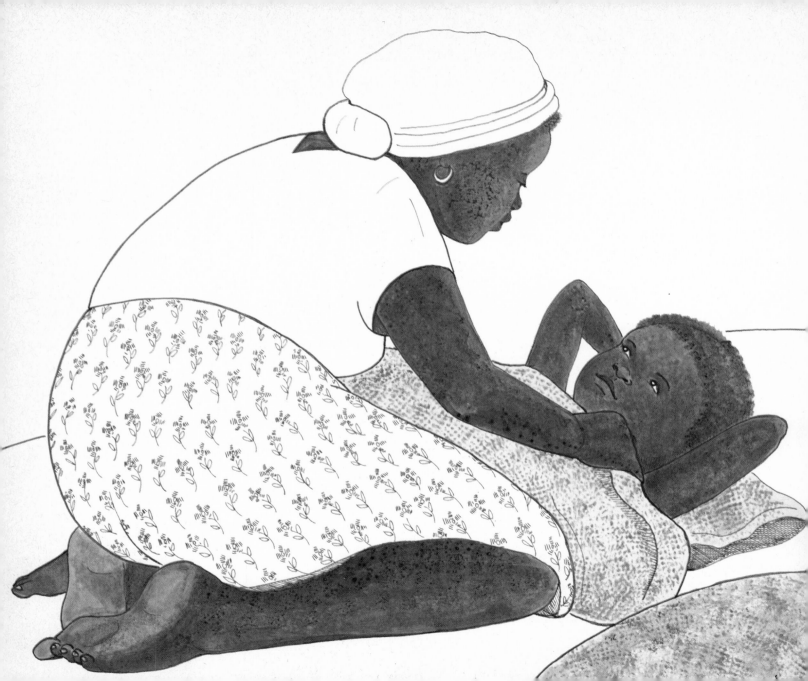

Then, as the blanket of night
spreads out over the world,
with a bright moon above,
my mother wraps us up carefully
and with a kiss and goodnight
puts us to sleep.

First published 1981 by Evans Brothers Limited,
Montague House, Russell Square, London WC1B 5BX
Reprinted 1982
Story © 1981 Hugh Lewin
Pictures © 1981 Lisa Kopper
British Library Cataloguing in Publication Data
Lewin, Hugh
Jafta – My mother – (Jafta's family series).
1. Africa – Social life and customs – Juvenile literature
2. Mothers – Africa – Juvenile literature
3. Villages – Africa – Juvenile literature
I. Title   II. Series
960'.0973'4   DT14
ISBN 0–237–45544–7
NPR 239
Made and printed in Great Britain by
Purnell and Sons (Book Production) Limited
Paulton, Bristol